TIME MANAGEMENT

TIME MANAGEMENT

BRIAN TRACY

AMACOM AMERICAN MANAGEMENT ASSOCIATION
New York · Atlanta · Brussels · Chicago · Mexico City
San Francisco · Shanghai · Tokyo · Toronto · Washington, D.C.

Library of Congress Cataloging-in-Publication Data

Tracy, Brian.
Time management / Brian Tracy.
    pages cm
Includes index.
ISBN-13: 978-0-8144-3343-0
ISBN-10: 0-8144-3343-X
1. Time management. I. Title.
HD69.T54T727 2014
650.1'1—dc23

                                                              2013037775

About AMA

American Management Association (www.amanet.org) is a world leader in talent development, advancing the skills of individuals to drive business success. Our mission is to support the goals of individuals and organizations through a complete range of products and services, including classroom and virtual seminars, webcasts, webinars, podcasts, conferences, corporate and government solutions, business books, and research. AMA's approach to improving performance combines experiential learning—learning through doing—with opportunities for ongoing professional growth at every step of one's career journey.

Printing number
10 9 8 7 6 5 4 3

CONTENTS

Introduction

YOUR ABILITY TO manage your time, as much as any other practice in your career as an executive, will determine your success or failure. Time is the one indispensable and irreplaceable resource of accomplishment. It is your most precious asset. It cannot be saved, nor can it be recovered once lost. Everything you have to do requires time, and the better you use your time, the more you will accomplish, and the greater will be your rewards.

Time management is essential for maximum health and personal effectiveness. The degree to which you feel in control of your time and your life is a major determinant of your level of inner peace, harmony, and mental well-being. A feeling of being "out of control" of your time is the major source of stress, anxiety, and depression. The better you can organize and control the critical events of your life, the better you will feel, moment to moment, the more energy you will have, the better you will sleep, and the more you will get done.

It is possible for you to gain two productive hours each working day, or even double your output and your productivity, by using the ideas and methods taught in this book. These techniques have proven successful for many thousands of executives in every field of endeavor, and they will prove successful for you, too, as long as you have what I call the four Ds.

The Four Ds of Effectiveness

The first D is *desire*: You must have an intense, burning desire to get your time under control and to achieve maximum effectiveness.

The second D is *decisiveness*: You must make a clear decision that you are going to practice good time management techniques until they become a habit.

The third D stands for *determination*: You must be willing to persist in the face of all temptations to the contrary until you have become an effective time manager. Your desire will reinforce your determination.

And finally, the most important key to success in life, the fourth D, is *discipline*: You must discipline yourself to make time management a lifelong practice. Effective discipline is the willingness to force yourself to pay the price, and to do what you know you should do, when you should do it, whether you feel like it or not. This is critical for success.

The payoff for becoming an excellent time manager is huge. It is the outwardly identifiable quality of a high performer vs. a low performer. All winners in life use their time well. All poor performers in life use their time poorly. One of the most important rules for success is simply to "form good habits and make them your masters." In this book, you will learn how to form good habits and then let them form you.

What you will learn in this book are the twenty-one most important solutions to effective time management that almost all highly productive people have discovered and incorporated into their lives.

Remember that time management is really life management. Good time management and personal productivity begins by valuing your life, and every minute of that life.

Do What You Can, with What You Have, Right Where You Are

You should say to yourself, "My life is precious and important, and I value every single minute and hour of it. I am going to use those hours properly so that I accomplish the most I can, in the time that I have."

The good news is that time management is a business skill, and all business skills are learnable. Time management is like riding a bicycle, typing on a keyboard, or playing a sport. It is made up of a series of methods, strategies, and techniques. It is a skill set that you can learn, practice, and master with determination and repetition.

ONE

The Psychology of Time Management

HOW YOU THINK and feel about yourself largely determines the quality of your life, and the emotional core of your personality is your self-esteem, defined as "how much you like yourself."

Your self-esteem is largely determined by the way you use your life and time in the development of your full potential. Your self-esteem increases when you are working efficiently, and your self-esteem goes down when you are not.

The flip side of the coin of self-esteem is called "self-efficacy," defined as the degree to which you feel you are competent, capable, and productive, able to solve your problems, do your work, and achieve your goals.

The more competent, capable, and productive you feel, the higher your self-esteem. The higher your self-esteem, the more productive and capable you will be. Each one supports and reinforces the other.

People who manage their time well feel positive, confident, and in charge of their lives.

The Law of Control

The psychology of time management is based on a simple principle called the Law of Control. This law says that you feel good about yourself to the degree to which you feel you are in control of your own life. This law also says that you feel negative about yourself to the degree to which you feel that you are not in control of your own life or work.

Psychologists refer to the difference between an *internal* locus of control, where you feel that you are the master of your own destiny, and an *external* locus of control, where you feel that you are controlled by circumstances outside yourself.

When you have an external locus of control, you feel that you are controlled by your boss and your bills, and by the pressure of your work and responsibilities. You feel that you have too much to do in too little time, and that you are not really in charge of your time and your life. Most of what you are doing, hour after hour, is reacting and responding to external events.

There is a big difference between *action* that is self-determined and goal-directed and *reaction*, which is an immediate response to external pressure. It's the difference between feeling positive and in control of your life and feeling negative, stressed, and pressured. To perform at your best, you must have a strong feeling of control in the important areas of your business and personal life.

Your Thoughts and Feelings

In psychological terms, each person has a self-concept, an internal master program that regulates his behavior in every important area of life. People with a high self-concept regarding time management see themselves and think about themselves as being well organized and productive. They are very much in charge of their lives and their work.

Your self-concept is made up of all of your ideas, pictures, images, and especially your beliefs about yourself, especially regarding the way you manage your time. Some people believe themselves to be extremely well organized and efficient. Others feel continuously overwhelmed by demands of other people and circumstances.

Beliefs Become Realities

What are your beliefs about yourself and your ability to manage your own time? Do you see yourself and think about yourself as a highly efficient and effective time manager? Do you believe you are highly productive and in complete control of your life and your work? Whatever your belief, if you think of yourself as an excellent time manager, you will naturally do those things that are consistent with that belief.

Because your self-concept causes you to continually strive for consistency between the person you see yourself as, on the inside, and the way you perform on the outside, if you believe you manage your time well, you will be a good time manager.

You can take all of the courses on time management, read all the books, and practice the various systems, but if you perceive yourself as being a poor time manager, nothing will help. If you have developed the habit of being late for meetings and appointments, or you believe that you are a disorganized person, those habits become your automatic behavior. If you do not change your beliefs about your personal levels of effectiveness and efficiency, your ability to manage your time will not change, either.

Make a Decision

How do you develop new, positive beliefs about yourself and your level of personal productivity? Fortunately, it is not difficult. You simply use the four Ds: desire, decisiveness, determination, and discipline. Most important, make a decision to develop a specific time management habit, like being early for every meeting for the foreseeable future. Every change in your life comes about when you make a clear, unequivocal decision to do something differently. Making the decision to become an excellent time manager is the first major step.

Program Your Mind

Once you have made the decision to become a highly productive person, there are a series of personal programming techniques that you can practice.

The first is to change your inner dialogue. Ninety-five percent of your emotions, and your eventual actions, are determined by the way that you talk to yourself most of the time. Repeat to yourself, "I am well organized and highly productive." Whenever you feel overwhelmed with too much work, take a time-out and say to yourself, "I am well organized and highly productive."

Affirm over and over to yourself that "I am an excellent time manager." If people ask you about your time usage, tell them "I am an excellent time manager."

Whenever you say that "I am well organized," your subconscious accepts these words as a command and begins to motivate and drive you toward actually becoming well organized in your behaviors.

Visualize Yourself as You Want to Be

The second way to transform your behaviors is to visualize yourself as an excellent time manager. See yourself as organized, efficient, and in control of your life. Remember, the person you "see" on the inside is the person you will "be" on the outside.

If you are already a well-organized and highly productive person, how would you behave differently? What would be different from the way you behave today? Create a picture of yourself as calm, confident, highly efficient, more relaxed, and able to complete large amounts of work in a short period of time.

Imagine what a highly productive person would look like. Would the person's desk be clear and tidy? Would the person appear unhurried and unstressed? Create a clear mental picture of yourself as a person who is in control of his time and life.

Act "As If"

The third way to program yourself is to act "as if" you were already a good time manager. Think of yourself as being well organized in everything you do. If you were already excellent in time management, how would you behave? What would you be doing differently? With regard to your time and personal productivity, what would be different from the way you do things now?

Interestingly enough, even if you do not think that you are a good time manager today, but nonetheless you *pretend* that you already are, these actions will generate a feeling of personal efficiency. You can actually change your actions, habits, and behavior when you "fake it until you make it."

TWO

Determine Your Values

SINCE TIME MANAGEMENT is really life management, improving your personal productivity begins with an examination of your values. One of Murphy's Laws says that before you do anything, you have to do something else first. It's not possible to manage your time properly unless you know exactly what your values are.

Good time management requires that you bring your control over a sequence of events into harmony with what is most important to you. If it is not important to you, then you will never feel motivated and determined to get control of your time.

Ask yourself this: "Why am I doing what I am doing?" Why do you get up in the morning? Why do you do the job you do? What is your reason for working where you work?

Meaning and Purpose

Each person has a deep need for meaning and purpose in life. One of the major reasons for personal stress and unhappiness is the feeling that what you are doing has no meaning and purpose as it applies to you and your innermost values and convictions. You must always start off by asking the question "Why?"

You can become more efficient with time management techniques, but it won't do you any good if you just become more efficient at doing something that is meaningless to you. Greater efficiency will simply increase your sense of alienation, frustration, and anxiety.

What Do You Value Most?

The next question you need to ask is, "What do you value most in life?" What do you really care about and stand for? What will you not stand for?

You will only feel really happy, valuable, and worthwhile to the degree to which your day-to-day activities are in harmony with your values. Almost all stress, tension, anxiety, and frustration, both in life and in work, comes from doing one thing while you believe and value something completely different.

There are many reports about executives experiencing burnout as the result of the stress of their work. But people who love what they are doing, and put their whole heart into their work because it is a reflection of their values, seldom experience stress or burnout of any kind. When you are living consistent with your values, you seem to experience a continuous flow of energy, enthusiasm, and creativity. Stress comes from working at things that are not consistent with your highest values.

Examine your values, your innermost beliefs and convictions, and ask yourself what changes you could make to bring your activities, on the outside, and your life priorities, on the inside, more into alignment with each other.

You Are Extraordinary

Realize and accept that you are a unique and wonderful person. Your values have grown and evolved over the course of your entire lifetime. They have emerged as the result of countless influences and experiences. They are part of your psychological and emotional DNA. They are part of your character and personality. They seldom change over time. Your job is to determine what your innermost values really are, and then to organize your life so that you are living and working consistent with those values.

Analyze Yourself

Here are four sentence completion exercises that you can use to gain better insight into the person you really are inside. Complete each sentence:

1. "*I am . . .*" If a stranger were to ask you, "Who are you, really?" what would be your answer? What are the first words that you would use to describe yourself? Would you describe

yourself in terms of your work, your qualities as a person, your hopes, dreams, and aspirations? Select three to five words to complete the sentence, "I am . . ."

If you were to interview the people around you, the people you live with and work with, and ask them the same question about yourself, what would they say? How would other people describe you in terms of your values and the person you really are? Based on the way you behave and treat other people, what conclusions would they come to about the person you are inside?

2. "*People are . . .*" Think of people in general, in the world around you. How would you describe the human race? Are people good, warm, and loving? Are people lazy, devious, or untrustworthy?

Your answer will have a major influence on how you treat other people in every part of your life. It will determine just about everything you will accomplish as an executive and as a person with family and friends.

3. "*Life is . . .*" Your response here may seem simple, but it speaks to your entire philosophy of life. Positive, healthy, happy people see life as a wonderful experience, full of ups and downs, but certainly a great adventure overall.

One of my favorite stories is about a young man who goes to an old philosopher and says, "Life is hard."

The philosopher replies, "As compared with what?"

As Helen Keller said, "Life is either a daring adventure or nothing at all." What is life to you?

4. "*My biggest goal in life is* . . ." If you could wave a magic wand and accomplish a single big goal in life, what one goal, either short or long term, would have the greatest positive impact on your life? Now, complete these sentences:

"My biggest goal in my career is . . ."

"My biggest goal for my family is . . ."

These are some of the most profound and important questions you can ever ask and answer for yourself. When you become clear about your answers—which will not be easy—you can then ask yourself what changes you would need to make to bring your time usage and your life priorities more into alignment with each other.

Napoleon Hill observed that life only begins to become great when we decide clearly upon our most important goal in life.

What are your most important goals?

Think About Your Vision and Mission

ONE OF THE BEST and most profound books written in the last few years is Daniel Kahneman's *Thinking, Fast and Slow*. His insight is that we need to use two different types of thinking to deal with the variety of situations we face in our daily lives.

Fast thinking is the type of thinking that we use to deal with short-term tasks, responsibilities, activities, problems, and situations. We act quickly and instinctively. In most cases, fast thinking is entirely appropriate for our day-to-day activities.

The second type of thinking that Kahneman describes is slow thinking. That's when you step back and take more time to carefully think through the details of the situation before deciding what you are going to do. Kahneman's insight is that the failure to engage in slow thinking when it is required and necessary is the cause of many of the mistakes that we make in life.

To become excellent in time management, and to get your entire life under control, you need to engage in "slow thinking" on a regular basis. Start with the question, "What am I trying to do?"

Think Before Acting

Very often you can find yourself working extremely hard at your work, but you have not taken the time to stand back and think about what it is you really want to accomplish.

There is the story of the husband and wife who leave on a car trip from San Diego to Los Angeles. He is unfamiliar with the road but driving at full speed in any case. At a certain point, the wife says, "Honey, is Phoenix on the way to Los Angeles?"

He then says, "Why do you ask?" She answers, "Well, we just passed a sign that said we are on the road to Phoenix."

He replies, "Never mind. We're making great time!"

Before you step on the accelerator of your own life, you must develop absolute clarity about what you are really trying to accomplish.

In *The Devil's Dictionary*, Ambrose Bierce wrote that "the definition of fanaticism is redoubling your efforts after your aim has been forgotten."

Is your goal to create a great life? Are you trying to build a great career or accomplish a great piece of work? Your ability to stand back and engage in self-analysis and introspection—slow thinking—is essential for you to organize your time in such a way that you are the most productive, and that you are achieving the greatest amount of joy, satisfaction, and happiness from what you do.

Keep the End in Mind

Be clear about what outcomes you desire. As Stephen Covey said, "Start with the end in mind." What is the final result, outcome, or accomplishment that you are striving to achieve? Where do you want to end up at the end of the day? As you scramble up the ladder of success, be sure that it is leaning against the right building.

Are you working so that you can earn enough money to be secure and to feel happy? Are you working because you love your work, or because you feel you're on a mission to accomplish something that is very important?

What would your world look like if you accomplished your biggest goal? What is your vision for yourself and your career over the long term? What is your mission? What difference do you want to make in the lives of other people?

If all you are working for is to earn enough money to pay your bills, it's going to be hard for you to build up and maintain a high level of commitment and enthusiasm. To be truly happy and fulfilled, you must be working toward accomplishing something that is bigger than yourself, and that makes a difference in the life or work of others.

Examine Your Methodology

When you are clear about what you are trying to do, you must then ask, "How am I trying to do it?" Each time you ask and answer these two questions, you will gain valuable insights that will allow you to look at your situation and know whether you are on the right track.

Once you are clear about what you are trying to do and how you are trying to do it, you must then ask a third question: "How is it going?"

Is what you are doing moving you toward what you want in the fastest and most efficient way? Are you happy with your rate of progress? Are things going well, or are you experiencing too many roadblocks and obstacles on your journey?

Most of all, question your assumptions. As Peter Drucker said, "Errant assumptions lie at the root of every failure."

What are your assumptions about your work and your life? What are your conscious assumptions? What are your unconscious and often unquestioned assumptions? It is amazing how many hardworking people are laboring on the basis of false assumptions that they have never questioned.

Seek a Better Way

As you ponder the "How's it going?" question, you should also be considering another important question: "Could there be a better way?"

The fact is that there is almost always a different and better way to achieve a business goal. This other way may be faster, cheaper, easier, and more effective.

There is a beautiful line that says, "There is more to life than just increasing its speed."

Many people are working very hard but going in the wrong direction on the wrong path. They are not clear about what they are trying to do and where they want to end up, but they don't want to face or deal with the possibility that they could be wrong. The process of asking tough questions requires slow thinking, but it can significantly increase the speed at which you achieve your business goals and your vision and mission.

FOUR

Project Forward, Look Backward

WHAT IS THE MOST important and valuable work that you do, in any field or profession? It's *thinking*! Your ability to think clearly about what you do and how you do it will have a greater impact on your future results than any other single action you take.

There are some areas of your work where "slow thinking" is absolutely essential for you to perform at your best.

Take thirty minutes or more each day to review your goals, your plans, and your progress. The best time to do this review is first thing in the morning. Take time to think, plan, dream, and create. All exceptional executives and highly effective men and women set aside this time each day to carefully consider what they are going to do before they begin. You should read, review, reflect, and think about what you are doing before you take action.

Over the years, I have read hundreds of biographies and autobiographies of successful men and women in every field. One common thread in these biographies that I discovered was that true greatness only emerges with introspection, retrospection, solitude, and contemplation. You will only achieve the greatness you are capable of when you begin to take time regularly to think about who you are, what you want, and the very best way to achieve it.

Take the time to evaluate your life and your activities in a larger context. Think of where you are today and where you want to be in five years. Look at the activities that you are engaged in today and determine which of them can have the greatest impact on your future. This way of thinking will allow you to manage your time much better than you can even imagine at this moment. Sometimes, just one good idea gained in a period of solitude or contemplation can save you months and even years of hard work.

Long Time Perspective

Dr. Edward Banfield of Harvard University conducted more than fifty years of research into the attitudes and behaviors of high-performing people, both in America and worldwide. He identified one special quality that seemed to separate the high performers from the low performers. He called it "long time perspective." Banfield found that high performers took the time to think far into the future, often ten and twenty years, and to develop absolute clarity about where they wanted to be in their lives and work at that time. They then come back to the present and make sure that everything they are doing in the moment is consistent with where they want to be in the future.

This is a powerful technique that you can use, too. Project forward one, two, or three years, and imagine that your life situation is ideal in every way. Create a clear mental picture of what your work situation would be if it were perfect. From this vantage point of the future, look around you and describe your ideal life and work situation. Then, ask yourself if what you are doing right now is consistent with the creation of your ideal future.

From that future vantage point, look back at yourself, to where you are today, and see the steps that you will need to take to get to where you want to go. This "back from the future thinking" is a practice of many top executives.

Make Better Decisions in the Present

For example, a young woman decides that she wants to be very successful in business in her adult life. With this clear long-term perspective in mind, the individual works many extra hours to get excellent grades in high school so that she will qualify for a good college. In college, the individual takes harder courses and studies much longer than her peers to graduate as close as possible to the top of her class.

As a result of many years of hard work and study, and putting off the immediate gratification of parties, sports, and social life, the individual graduates at a high level from a prestigious university and is then hired by a large company, where she has the opportunity to get paid more and promoted faster than classmates who were not really thinking about the future at all.

When you are clear about where you want to be sometime in the future, it is much easier for you to make better decisions in the present. The rule is that long-term vision improves short-term decision making. You have heard the saying, "If you don't know where you're going, any road will get you there."

The habit of developing long time perspective is quite powerful. By projecting into the future and looking back to the present, you will often see steps that you could take, and mistakes that you could avoid. This exercise will help you to crystallize your values. It will give you the internal tools to organize your time and activities so that what you are doing today is moving you toward the creation of your ideal future.

Ready for Time Management Techniques

If you are not headed toward your desired destination, you don't want to get there any faster. If you are not moving in your own self-determined direction, there is no point in managing your time in a way that accelerates your speed of accomplishment. Time management strategies and tactics applied without a clear future vision will get you to a destination that holds no interest for you, only faster.

Once you are clear about your values, vision, and mission for your life and work, and you are clear about what it is you want to accomplish and the best way to achieve it, then, and only then, can you begin to apply some of the powerful time management techniques that are available to you.

FIVE

Make Written Plans

ALL SUCCESSFUL TIME managers are good planners. They make lists and sublists to accomplish each major and minor objective. Whenever a new project crosses their desk, they take the time to think through exactly what they want to accomplish, and then write out an orderly list, in sequence, of every step necessary for the completion of the project.

There is a rule that every minute spent in planning saves ten minutes in execution. The time you take to think on paper about something you need to accomplish, before you begin work, will give you a return on personal energy of 1,000 percent—ten minutes saved for every minute that you invest in planning your work in the first place.

Once you are clear about your goal, you then make a list of everything that you can think of that you will have to do to achieve that goal. Keep adding new items to the list as you think of them, until your list is complete. Organize your list two ways: by sequence and by priority.

First, in organizing by sequence, you create a list of activities in chronological order, from the first step to the final step before completion of the goal or project. As Henry Ford said, "The biggest goal can be achieved if you simply break it down into enough small parts."

Second, you set priorities on these items, accepting that 20 percent of the items on your list will account for 80 percent of the value and importance of all the things you do. Setting priorities allows you to stay focused on your key tasks and activities without getting distracted. As Goethe said, "The things that matter most must never be at the mercy of the things that matter least."

Review your plans regularly, especially when you experience frustration or resistance of any kind. Be prepared to revise your plans when you receive new information or feedback. Remember that almost every plan has flaws in it, both large and small. Continually seek them out. When you review your plans daily, you will get new ideas, perspectives, and insights about how to complete the task faster and better than you may have thought initially.

Action without planning is the cause of every failure. Resist the temptation to take action before you have planned it out thoroughly in advance.

Planning for Goal Achievement

Perhaps the most important word related to success of any kind is *clarity*. Successful people are very clear about who they are and what they want, in every area of their lives. In addition to written goals, successful people have written plans of action that they follow every day.

Once you have set a larger goal for yourself and your business, there are four questions that you should ask:

1. *What are the difficulties and obstacles that stand between you and the achievement of your goal?* Why aren't you at your goal already? What is holding you back? What stands in your way? What problems do you have to solve, what difficulties do you have to overcome, to achieve your goal in the end?

Of all the problems you need to solve, what are the 20 percent of the problems that account for 80 percent of the obstacles between you and your goal?

2. *What additional knowledge, skills, or information are required to achieve your goal or complete your project?* Remember the saying, "Whatever got you to where you are today is not enough to get you any further."

Where can you acquire the additional knowledge and skills that you need to achieve your goal? Can you buy or hire the knowledge or information? Do you need to develop new skills in yourself in order to achieve your full potential in your work? What information is essential to you in making the right decisions in the process of achieving your goal?

As Josh Billings wrote, "It's not what a man knows that hurts him; it's what he knows that isn't true."

3. *Who are the people, groups, or organizations whose help and cooperation you need in order to achieve your goal?* Sometimes, a single person can give you ideas and insights or open doors for you, helping you to achieve vastly more than you ever thought possible. It's the same reason many businesspeople enter into joint ventures and strategic alliances with their competitors in order to offer products and services to each other's customers that each of them does not currently offer.

4. *Of all the people who can help you to achieve your goal, who is the most important person of all?* What could you offer in exchange to gain this person's help and cooperation so that you achieve your important goals even faster?

The most important projects in business, and in the world around us, are completed by people who make detailed plans of action before they begin. Make written plans for yourself and your business, and then follow those plans carefully until they are successful.

SIX

Chart Your Projects

MOST WORK IN business is a series of projects. Your ability to complete projects largely determines your success in your career. A project is defined as a "multitask job." A project is a result that requires the completion of a series of many smaller jobs.

Perhaps the most powerful tool you can use to maximize your effectiveness and dramatically increase your level of accomplishment is a *checklist*. A checklist consists of a written series of steps, in chronological order, which you create in advance of beginning work in the first place.

Your ability to clearly define and determine the steps that you will have to take from where you are today to a successfully completed project is a mark of superior thinking. The rule, once again, is that every minute spent in planning and creating checklists will save you ten minutes in execution and getting the job done. This is another example of slow thinking that can significantly increase your effectiveness and your output, and your ultimate value to your business.

Create a PERT Chart

Create a visual representation of your larger tasks and projects so that you and others can see it in its totality.

Begin by determining the goals and objectives you must achieve to enjoy the outcomes you desire. Start with the end in mind. Take the time to develop absolute clarity about what your goals would look like if they were accomplished in an excellent fashion. Then, work back from the future to the present. Make a list of the logical steps, in order, that you need to take to get from where you are to where you want to be.

The use of a PERT chart (which stands for Program Evaluation Review Technique) sets out graphically all the steps you need to take and when each one needs to be finished for you to achieve the final goal. This technique is used by the most efficient and effective companies and executives worldwide. A PERT chart enables you to see a variety of ways to achieve the task with greater efficiency.

There are many forms and styles available online for you to choose from. One example is depicted in Figure 1.

To create the chart, for each of your objectives or goals, draw a line plotted backward from the required date of completion. Lay it out on paper so that you can see when you

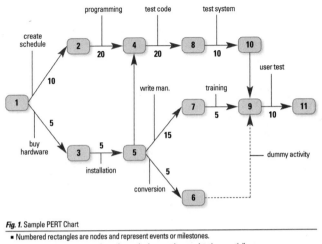

Fig. 1. Sample PERT Chart

- Numbered rectangles are nodes and represent events or milestones.
- Directional arrows represent dependent tasks that must be completed sequentially.
- Diverging arrow directions (e.g., 1–2 and 1–3) indicate possibly concurrent tasks.
- Dotted lines indicate dependent tasks that do not require resources.

have to accomplish each part of the task in order to have the entire job completed on schedule.

By thinking on paper and using a PERT chart, you take complete control of the sequence of events. You have a track to run on. You have a series of tasks that you can check on to be sure that they are completed on schedule and to a satisfactory level of quality. By using a PERT chart, you avoid being overwhelmed by deadlines. You are always on top of your work and your major projects.

If you need something done by the end of the month, you can set your time line with plenty of cushion at the fifteenth or twentieth of the month, just in case unexpected delays or problems arise. Always remember Murphy's Law: "Whatever can go wrong will go wrong."

The superior executive assumes that there will be problems, obstacles, unexpected delays, and failures to complete the job by the agreed-on schedule. These occurrences are a normal and natural part of business life. Your job is to keep your finger on the pulse of the project continually, and then to solve the problems and remove the obstacles that are bound to arise. Once you begin using a PERT chart, however, you may be quite amazed at how much more you accomplish and how many fewer hiccups or conflicts there will be between the steps.

Set Clear Goals for Everyone

You will accomplish more with clear, written goals for each key person involved in the project than you ever could with great conversations and good intentions. Make goals clear, specific, measurable, and time bounded. Remember that what gets measured gets done. A goal without a deadline is not really a goal. It is merely a discussion.

For every goal or subgoal in the completion of a job or project, you must assign responsibility to a specific person. Who is going to perform this task? When does the task need to be completed, and to what standard of quality? Always ask these questions. Never assume that people know what you want unless you have made it perfectly clear.

General Motors went from massive losses and bankruptcy in 2009 to a $4.9 billion profit in 2012. Dan Akerson, the president of GM, said that the most important part of the company's turnaround was the setting of clear goals for each key person and at each level of the organization. Before taking the position, he found that goals throughout the organization were vague, unclear, unenforced, and rarely achieved. After establishing clear, specific goals, all employees knew exactly what they had to do to keep their job and to move ahead.

Remember, the most wonderful talent you have is your ability to think, especially to think things through in advance. The more time you take to think and plan, on paper, the better results you will get, and the faster you will get those results.

SEVEN

Create Your Daily "To-Do" List

PERHAPS THE MOST powerful time management tool is a daily list of activities that you create to serve as a blueprint for your day.

All successful time managers think on paper and work from a daily list of activities. Just as a pilot uses a checklist before every takeoff, effective executives take a few minutes to create a "to-do" list before they begin each day.

The best time to make a list is the night before, so your subconscious mind can work on your list while you sleep. When you wake up in the morning, you will often have ideas and insights to help you achieve some of the most important goals on your list.

At the end of each day, the last thing you do should be to plan out the next day. In a study of more than fifty highly effective corporate executives, forty-nine of the fifty said that the best time management system they had ever found was a simple pad of paper on which they wrote down everything they had to do before they began.

Sleep Better

Many people toss and turn at night trying not to forget something they have to do the following day. If you create a list before you go to bed, writing down everything you have planned for the coming workday, you will sleep far better and awake more refreshed.

According to time management specialists, it takes about twelve minutes each day to write out a list of your tasks for that day. But this list will save you ten times that amount of time in improved productivity. Twelve minutes spent in preparing a daily list will give you a payback of 120 minutes, or two hours of increased productivity, when you actually begin work. That's an incredible payoff for such a simple task.

The ABCDE Method

Once you have made up a list of everything that you plan to do the next day, organize your list by applying the ABCDE method to your activities.

The most important word in time management is *consequences*. A task is important depending on the potential consequences of doing it or not doing it. When you set priorities, you apply this principle to every task, and you always begin with the task that has the greatest consequences. This is where the ABCDE method is especially helpful.

Begin by making a list of everything you have to do the following day. Then, write an A, B, C, D, or E next to each item on your list before you begin work.

An item that's marked A is something you *must do*. It is something that is important and there are serious consequences for either doing it or not doing it. Put an A next to those tasks and activities that you must accomplish in the course of the day if you are to fulfill your responsibilities.

B items are those things you *should do*. There are mild consequences for doing (or not doing) B tasks, but they are not as important as A activities. The rule is that you never do a B activity when there is an A activity left undone.

C activities are *nice to do*, but they have no consequences, either positive or negative. Chatting with a coworker, getting an extra cup of coffee, or checking your e-mail are things that are nice to do, and often fun and enjoyable, but whether or not you do them has no consequences at all in terms of your effectiveness at your job.

Time Wastage Sabotages Careers

Robert Half International estimates that as much as 50 percent of working time is spent on C activities, things that make no contribution at all to the business.

Each person is a creature of habit. Effective people establish good habits and make them their masters. Ineffective people accidentally establish bad habits, and then those bad habits govern their lives.

Many people get into the habit of coming in to work and immediately engaging in time-wasting, low-value, no-value activities. As soon as they arrive, they find someone to chat with, read the newspaper, check their e-mail, get a cup of coffee, and generally begin coasting easily through the day.

But whatever you do repeatedly soon becomes a *habit*. It is unfortunate that the great majority of people at work today have established the habit of wasting most of their time on activities that contribute nothing to their businesses or to their careers. Don't let this happen to you.

Delegate Everything Possible

Getting back to the ABCDE method, a D activity is something that you can *delegate* to someone else. The rule is that you should delegate everything that you possibly can to other people to free up more time for you to engage in your A activities. Your A activities, and their successful completion, largely determine the entire course of your career.

An E activity is something that you should *eliminate* altogether. After all, you can only get your time under control if you stop doing things that are no longer necessary for you to do.

It is normal and natural for people to slip into a comfort zone in the course of their work and career. They become comfortable doing certain activities in a certain way. Even after they have been promoted to higher-level responsibilities, they continually slip back into doing things that are no longer really necessary, or that other people could do equally as well, or better.

Ask yourself, "What would happen if I did not engage in this activity at all?" If it would make little or no difference to your business or career, it is a prime candidate for elimination.

Plan Your Work and Work Your Plan

Never do anything that is not on your list. If a new task or project comes up, write it down on your list and set a priority for it before you start work on it. If you don't write down new ideas and activities, and instead react and respond to the nonstop demands on your time, you will quickly lose control of your day and end up spending most of your time on activities of low or no value.

Any time management system is better than no time management system at all. There are many smartphone apps to help you manage your time. There are time management systems that you can install on your computer. You can use a written time management system that you carry with you and update regularly.

Just remember that in the world of work, the only thing you have to sell is your time. Be sure that you are focusing your time on the most valuable and important things that you can do to make the most important contribution to your business.

The Not-To-Do List

Just as you need a to-do list to guide you through a busy day, you need a not-to-do list to help keep you on track. These are things that you decide, in advance, that you are not going to do, no matter how tempting they may be when they come up.

As Nancy Reagan once said, "Just say no!" Just say no to any activity that does not represent the highest value of your time.

"No" is the greatest time-saving word in the world of time management. And once you start using this word, it gets easier and easier to say.

Remember, *people* are the greatest time wasters of all. When people ask you if you would do something or help them out in some way, ask yourself, "Would this be the most valuable use of my time, right now?"

If the answer is "no," you can graciously reply, "Well, thank you for asking. Let me think about it and look at my schedule. I'll get back to you and let you know whether or not I can help you out."

You can wait twenty-four hours, then contact the person and say that, unfortunately, you are swamped with work and deadlines at this point, and you won't be able to help out. Thank the person for asking for your assistance, and suggest that "maybe next time" you will have an opening on your calendar.

Remember, you can only get your time under control if you stop doing things of low value. As they say, your dance card is already full. You already have vastly more work than you can ever get done. You will never get caught up on your current tasks and responsibilities, let alone the additional tasks and responsibilities that flow to you every single day. Instead, just say no. Say it early and say it often. In no time at all, you will have your time completely under your own control.

EIGHT

Set Clear Priorities

I HAVE STUDIED time management for more than thirty years, reading hundreds of books and articles on the subject, listening to countless audio programs, and attending seminars. Using the ideas that I have assembled, I have written books of my own on time management that are worldwide bestsellers, produced audio and video learning programs, and conducted seminars and workshops on time management all over the world.

What I discovered was simple: All of time management boils down to helping you determine the most important task that you can do at the moment, and then giving you the tools and techniques to begin immediately with that one task, so you can keep working on it until it is complete.

I explained the ABCDE method in the last chapter. It is one of the most powerful priority-setting methods ever discovered. There are a series of additional techniques that you can also use to set priorities.

The Pareto Principle

In 1895, Italian economist Vilfredo Pareto concluded that the 80/20 rule seemed to apply to money, property, and the accumulation of fortunes in every society. After years of research, he discovered that 20 percent of individuals and families—those he called the "vital few"—controlled 80 percent of the wealth and property throughout Europe.

The 80/20 rule seems to apply to almost all areas of human endeavor, especially tasks and responsibilities. That is, 20 percent of the work that you do will account for 80 percent of the value of all the work that you do. Peter Drucker says that often it is the "90/10 rule." Sometimes 10 percent of the work that you do will account for 90 percent of the value.

When you start off each day with a list of your tasks and responsibilities, before beginning work, quickly review your list and select the top 20 percent of tasks that can make the greatest contribution to achieving your most important goals and objectives. If you have a list of ten items to accomplish on a particular day, two of those items will be worth more than all the others put together.

Your ability to clearly identify those two items and act on them first will largely determine your success in your career.

Put on the Pressure

Here's another technique that you can use for setting priorities: Make up your daily list of activities and then ask yourself, "If I were called out of town for a month, starting tomorrow, what activities on this list would I want to be sure to complete before I left town?"

The greatest enemy of time management and personal productivity today is "majoring in minors." Because of the natural tendency for each person to follow the path of least resistance and to settle into a comfort zone, it is normal and natural for people to begin with small, easy, fun, enjoyable, and usually unimportant tasks and activities at the beginning of the day.

But alas, whatever you start doing at the beginning of the day quickly becomes the pattern that you will follow in the hours ahead. By the end of the day, you may find that you have spent all of your time on small and meaningless tasks, and you will have accomplished nothing of real value.

Get More Important Things Done

Another technique you can use is to imagine that you come into work on Monday morning and your boss approaches you with a dilemma. He has just won a fully paid vacation for two people, with first-class airfare, to a beautiful resort. His problem is that he is too busy to take advantage of this prize, but it is time dated. It must be used starting first thing tomorrow morning.

Your boss makes you a deal. If you can get all of your most important work done by the end of Monday, he will give you and your spouse this wonderful, all-expenses-paid vacation.

If you had this kind of incentive or motivation, what would you do? You would probably be astonished at how much work you could get done in that single day. You would probably complete the top 20 percent of the tasks that you had planned for the entire week.

With that kind of an incentive, you would not waste a single minute. You would have no time at all for idle conversation with your coworkers. You would start early and immediately work through coffee breaks and lunch and concentrate single-mindedly on clearing your desk by completing your most important tasks. You would become one of the most productive people in your organization, virtually overnight.

This is a great exercise for you to practice on yourself. This exercise just illustrates the fact that your efficiency and effectiveness is largely a matter of choice. With a sufficient incentive, you would be astonished at how productive you could be, virtually in a few minutes. With a sufficient incentive, and a decision on your part, you would almost immediately become one of the most valuable people in your organization.

The Law of Three

This principle is probably worth the cost and time of reading this book. It is based on an amazing discovery that I have made over the years, working with many thousands of executives and business owners. It is that, no matter how many different things you do in a week or a month, there are only *three* tasks and activities that account for 90 percent of the value of the contribution you make to your business.

If you make a list of everything you do in the course of a month, it will probably include twenty, thirty, or even forty different tasks and responsibilities. But if you review that list carefully, item by item, you will find that only three items on your entire list account for 90 percent of your value to your business.

How do you determine your "big three"? Simple. Make a list of all your work tasks and responsibilities, from the first day of the month to the last day, and throughout the year. Then, answer these three magic questions.

1. *If I could only do one thing on this list, all day long, which one activity would contribute the greatest value to my business?* Your most important task—the one that accounts for the greatest contribution you can make to your business—will probably pop out at you from the list. It will usually be quite clear to you, as it is clear to the people around you. Put a circle around that item.

2. *If I could only do two things on this list, all day long, what would be the second activity that would make the greatest contribution to my business?* Usually, this item will jump out at you as well. It may require a little bit more thought, but it is usually clear and obvious.

3. *If I could only do three things on this list, all day long, what would be the third activity that would contribute the* *most value to my business?* When you analyze your answers, you will clearly see that only three things you do account for almost all the value that you contribute. Starting and completing these tasks is more important than everything else you do.

Here's an important point: If you do not know the answers to these three questions, you are in serious trouble. You are in great danger of wasting your time and your life at work. If you do not know the answer to these magic questions, you will always end up working on lower-value and often no-value activities.

If you are unclear for any reason, go to your boss. Ask what your boss thinks are the three most important things that you do to make your most valuable contribution at work. Ask your coworkers. Ask your spouse. But whatever you do, you must know the answers to these three questions.

Pass It Along

Once you are clear about your "big three," you must help all the people who report to you gain clarity about their "big three" as well. There is no kinder or more generous thing that you can do for your staff members than to help them become absolutely clear about the most important things that they do to make the most valuable contribution to your business.

In a well-managed department or organization, employees know exactly what the most important things are that they could do to make the greatest contribution. At the same time, every worker should know what every other worker's big three are. All day, every day, everyone should work, both alone and together, to complete one or more of those three big tasks.

People who are dominated by "fast thinking" naturally react and respond to the demands and pressures of the moment. They continually veer off track and away from working on their highest-priority tasks. But this practice is not for you.

Before you begin work, take some time to think slowly, select your most important task, and then start work on that task to the exclusion of everything else.

NINE

Stay on Track

"WHAT IS THE most valuable use of my time right now?"

Because it is the most important question in all of time management, ask it over and over again until it becomes an automatic guide that motivates and drives you to focus on your highest-value task or activity. When you organize all of your time and work activities around the answer to this question, you will be astonished at how much more productive you become, and how quickly.

Sometimes I ask my audiences, "What is your most valuable financial asset?"

After they have thought it over and given me a couple of answers, I point out that the answer is actually "your earning ability." Your ability to earn money represents as much as 80 percent to 90 percent of your financial value in the world of work.

Think of yourself as an "earning machine." Every task that you work on contributes a value of some kind, either high or low. Your job is to focus on the most valuable use of your time and to discipline yourself to continually work on those few activities that contribute the greatest value to your work and to your business.

A Lifestyle Principle

This selection of the most valuable use of your time applies to every area of your life as well. Sometimes, the most valuable use of your time, especially if you are working extremely hard, is to go home and go to bed early and get a good night's sleep. Sometimes the most valuable use of your time is to spend it face-to-face with the important people in your life. Sometimes the most valuable use of your time is to take excellent care of your physical health, by eating the right foods, taking time to get exercise regularly, and getting the proper rest and relaxation that you need to perform at your best.

Sometimes the most valuable use of your time is just to spend it with your family or to read a good book rather than watching television. At other times, the most valuable use of your time will be to socialize; to get together with family and friends whose company you enjoy so that you can relax and de-stress.

What matters most is for you to always be asking yourself this question: "What is the most valuable use of my time *right now*?" And then you discipline yourself to start and complete that activity, whatever it is. When you begin to incorporate this one suggestion into your time management skills and your day, you will become one of the most efficient time managers of your generation.

The Important vs. the Urgent

In terms of your tasks and activities, setting priorities is largely about separating the "vital few" from the "trivial many." There are four different types of tasks that you are faced with every day. Your ability to sort out these tasks into their proper categories can significantly increase your productivity. Each of these tasks can be put into a different box or quadrant.

QUADRANT 1: URGENT AND IMPORTANT

An *important* task is something that has long-term consequences for your career. An *urgent* task is something that cannot be delayed or put off. A task that is both urgent and important is something that is "in your face." It is largely determined by external demands on your time, by tasks and responsibilities that you must start and complete in order to keep on top of your job. There are people you have to see, things that you have to do, and places that you have to go. There are customers to visit, tasks to complete, and activities that others are expecting you to accomplish. Most people spend most of their working day on tasks that are both vital and urgent.

Your most important tasks, your highest priorities, are both urgent and important. This is called the "quadrant of immediacy."

QUADRANT 2: IMPORTANT, BUT NOT URGENT

The second type of tasks are those that are important but not urgent. They can be delayed or procrastinated upon, at least for the short term. An example of a task that is vital but not urgent is an important report that you must have written, approved, and submitted by the end of the month. Or think about a college term paper. It is something that is vital to your grade at the end of the semester, but it is also something that can be put off for weeks and months, and often is. (Most term papers are written the night before the deadline. What was at one time vital but not urgent suddenly becomes very urgent indeed.)

Throughout your life, you are surrounded by important but not urgent tasks. Reading important books in your field, taking additional courses, upgrading your skills and abilities are all vital to your long-term success, but they are not urgent. So, you procrastinate doing them. Most people who fail or underachieve in business have unfortunately put off upgrading their skills and abilities for so long that they are simply passed over and surpassed by other, more determined and aggressive people who want to enjoy greater rewards and responsibilities.

Even something as simple as physical exercise is vital to your health, but not urgent. You can put it off for an extended period of time, and most people do. Doctors say that 85 percent of the major health problems that people have later in life could have been avoided if they had engaged in proper health habits, including diet and exercise, for most of their adult lives. These tasks fall into the "quadrant of effectiveness."

QUADRANT 3: URGENT, BUT NOT IMPORTANT

You probably have people coming into your office, calling or messaging you, sending you e-mails, but your responses to them contribute little or no value to your business or your work. They represent tasks that are urgent but not important.

These tasks fall into what is often called the "quadrant of delusion." People think that because they are engaging in these activities during the working day, they must have some value, but they are just kidding themselves into career irrelevance. Many people spend as much as half of their time engaging in activities that are urgent but not important. They are fun, easy, and enjoyable, but they make no contribution to the work at all. Most of these activities involve idle conversation with coworkers, or low-value/no-value activities.

QUADRANT 4: NOT URGENT AND NOT IMPORTANT

The fourth type of activity that people engage in at work are those tasks that are neither urgent nor important. These activities fall into the "quadrant of waste." Many people engage in activities that have zero value to either themselves or the company. Reading e-mail spam or reading the sports pages, going shopping during the day, or driving around between appointments listening to the radio—all are examples of activities that are neither urgent nor important. They are a complete waste of time. They contribute nothing to your life.

Develop Good Work Habits

The great tragedy is that if you do something repeatedly, you soon develop a habit. And a habit, once formed, is hard to break. Many people have developed the habit of spending most of their time on low-value/no-value activities and then are quite astonished when they are laid off from their jobs or passed over for promotion.

The key to good time management is for you to set priorities and to always be working on what is both urgent and important—that is, your most pressing and important tasks. Once you are caught up with your tasks that are urgent and important, you immediately start work on those tasks that are important but not urgent at the moment. The tasks that are important but not urgent are usually those tasks and activities that can contribute to your career in a meaningful way in the long term.

TEN

Determine Your Key Result Areas

PERHAPS THE MOST important key to high productivity is for you to focus and concentrate on the most valuable and important things you can do, all day long.

Developing absolute clarity about your key result areas is essential for executive effectiveness and high productivity. Your key result areas are those things that you have been hired to do, accomplish, or achieve. They are your top priorities in terms of the value that you contribute to your business. These are the tasks that, once accomplished, determine whether or not you fulfill your responsibilities to your company and to yourself.

What are the key results that you have been hired to accomplish? Try asking the question another way: "Why are you on the payroll?" This is a key organizing question that you should be asking yourself every minute of every day—especially when you are overwhelmed by too much to do and too little time.

A key result area (KRA) can be defined as having three specific qualities:

1. It is something that you absolutely, positively must do to fulfill the responsibilities and demands of your job.

2. It is something for which you are 100 percent responsible. If you do not do it yourself, there is no one else who can or will do it for you.

3. It is something that is completely under your control. You do not need the assistance or participation of someone else in order to complete this part of your work.

If you are not sure exactly what your key result areas might be, go to your boss and ask. Ask your boss, "Why, exactly, am I on the payroll?"

Surprisingly enough, most bosses won't know how to answer this question, either. They have never thought through why you are on the payroll, or even why they themselves are on the payroll. When you ask this question and force your boss to think it through, you will both become more productive and effective in your work.

Keep on Track

A second question with regard to key result areas is: "What can only I do that, if done really well, will make a real difference to my organization?"

As it happens, there is a specific answer to this question for virtually every hour of every day.

In your work, there are things that only you can do. If you don't do them, no one else will do them for you. If you do them well, it will make an extraordinary difference to your job and to your company. These are the specific activities that contribute the greatest value to your work. For you to perform at the highest level, you must be absolutely clear about what those activities are that are more valuable than any others, and which only you can perform to distinction.

Remember, there are always a hundred little things that you can do that, if done well, will make very little difference to your success or to your contributions.

Focusing on key result areas is the most direct way to unleash effectiveness, power, persuasion, enthusiasm, and energy. You always get a tremendous feeling of self-confidence and personal power from completing something that is significant and important both to you and your company.

On the other hand, in the age of distraction, you actually experience feelings of low self-esteem, frustration, stress, and often depression when you are doing something that, in your heart of hearts, you know makes very little difference to achieving your major goals.

Define Your Key Result Areas

There are seldom more than five to seven key result areas in any job. Each KRA is a specific task that you must do if you are to complete the overall output responsibilities of your work.

For example, if you are a salesperson, your key result areas are:

1. Prospecting (i.e., finding new customers to talk to)

2. Building trust and rapport with prospects so that they are open to listening to you

3. Identifying needs accurately

4. Presenting your product persuasively

5. Answering objections clearly

6. Closing the sale decisively

7. Getting resales and referrals from satisfied customers

Each of these tasks must be done in order for you to fulfill your responsibilities as a salesperson for your company.

As a manager, you have seven key result areas as well. They are:

1. Planning (deciding exactly what is to be done)

2. Organizing (bringing together the people, money, and resources needed to fulfill the plan)

3. Recruiting (finding the right people to work with you to achieve the goals)

4. Delegating (making sure that people know exactly what they are supposed to do, and at what time, and to what level of quality)

5. Supervising (making sure that each job is done on schedule to the required level of quality)

6. Measuring (setting standards and benchmarks, plus time lines, for the accomplishment of important tasks)

7. Reporting (making sure that each person above you, next to you, and below you knows exactly what it is that you are doing and achieving)

More than 90 percent of all of your problems in management, or in life, are from "dropping the ball" in one of these key result areas. It is like leaving out an important ingredient in a kitchen recipe. For some reason, the dish simply does not taste as good as it could.

Clarity Is Essential

Everyone at every level of the organization should know what his or her key results are. Be sure that all employees who report to you are clear about the most valuable contribution that they can make to the organization. One of the greatest kindnesses that you can give to your employees is to help them to be crystal-clear about the most valuable and important things that they can do, and then to help them achieve those goals on time.

No matter where you are in your organization chart, you need to know two things: First, what are your boss's key result areas? What is it that your boss has to accomplish that is more important to the success of the organization than anything else? If you don't know the answers to these questions, you cannot help your boss get his or her job done, which is very important to your own personal success.

Second, you need to know what your own key result areas are. Furthermore, each person who reports to you must know the answer to this question about you as well. Each of your subordinates must also know what their key result areas are, in order of importance, and when they need to be accomplished.

ELEVEN

Delegate to Others

ONE OF THE GREATEST time management tools is for you to get someone else to do the task completely. Your ability to delegate lower-value tasks to others who can do them at a lower hourly rate or salary is one of the vital skills of modern management.

Delegate everything you possibly can to others who can do the tasks as well as or better than you. Use the "70 percent rule." If someone else can do a particular task 70 percent as well as you, this job is a prime candidate for you to get off your plate and on to that person's plate.

Multiply Your Value

Delegation enables you to move from what you can do personally to what you can manage. Delegation is the skill that allows you to leverage your talent and skill and multi-ply it *times* all the people who can be given smaller parts of the work.

You always have a choice. You can do it yourself, or you can have someone else do it. High productivity requires that you always think in terms of the latter approach: "Who else can do this job rather than me?"

Delegation Is Learnable

Learn the skills of proper delegation. (I have written an entire minibook in this series that tells you everything you need to know to maximize your productivity through other people.) Choose the right person to handle each task. Provide time lines, deadlines, standards of performance, and a review schedule.

You can also delegate problem solving and decision making if they are among your duties and responsibilities. You can delegate information gathering and research. You can delegate every task that anyone else can do as well as (or almost as well as) you.

With the skill of delegation, which is readily learnable, there is no limit that you cannot reach in your professional career. But without the ability to delegate efficiently and well, you will always end up with too much to do and too lit-tle time. You will end up doing too many things of low value or no value. You will never get caught up and on top of your job. And this can hurt your career.

The best news is that all business skills are learnable. Every idea in this book is something that you can master with practice and repetition. You can become absolutely excellent at managing your time and go on to double and triple your productivity in the months and years ahead.

TWELVE

Concentrate Single-Mindedly

CONCENTRATION AND single-handling are essential requirements for all great achievement. Concentration means that once you start on your most important task, you resolve to persevere without diversion or distraction. Your ability to concentrate single-mindedly on the most important use of your time is the number-one requirement for success.

You could meet every other requirement with intelligence, ability, and creativity, but if you cannot concentrate on one thing at a time, then you cannot be successful. You need to do first things first, one thing at a time, and second things not at all. If you do not discipline yourself to concentrate single-mindedly, you will invariably find yourself working on low-priority tasks.

Always allow enough time for your top priorities. Figure out how much time it is going to take to do the job and then add 30 percent as a cushion, to take into account unexpected interruptions, emergencies, and responsibilities. With a 30 percent cushion, you will probably be quite close to correct in your estimate of the time necessary to do the work. This is one of the secrets to achieving high levels of productivity in your work.

Earl Nightingale said that "every great accomplishment in life has been preceded by a long, sustained period of concentration."

Practice Single-Handling

Single-handling is one of the most important of all time management techniques and life management principles. Once you start a task, you stay with it until it is 100 percent complete. Single-handling requires that you do not continue picking up and putting down the same task, over and over, going off to something else and then coming back. With single-handling, once you pick up a task and begin on it, you discipline yourself to bring it to completion before you go on to the next task.

Apply single-handling to your mail and correspondence. Deselect unimportant items immediately and then deal with the important documents only once, either by filing or responding to them right away.

The principle of single-handling—made famous by time management expert Alan Lakein—comes from time and motion studies comparing the output of people who concentrated single-mindedly vs. the output of people who went back and forth on a task, going away and returning to that task many times in the course of task completion. What these studies found was that each time you put down a task and turn to something else, you lose momentum and rhythm, and you lose track of where you were in doing that job. When you come back to the task, you have no choice but to review your previous work, catch up to the point where you were when you broke off, and then begin again. This process turns out to require as much as 500 percent of the amount of time otherwise necessary to complete a task if you had started with it and stayed with it until it was 100 percent complete.

In simple terms, single-handling can reduce the time you spend completing an important task by as much as 80 percent, and dramatically increase the quality of the finished work.

Avoid Multitasking

There is a good deal of argument today over the concept of multitasking. Some people feel that they are quite capable of performing at high levels of productivity while they are working on several tasks at once. The studies have now proven that this idea is totally false.

What the experts have discovered is that multitasking is actually "task-shifting." The fact is that you can only do one thing at a time. If you stop doing one task to turn to another task, you must shift all of your attention and energy to the new task. When you turn back to the previous task, you are simply making a shift of attention, like pointing a light beam from one target to another. Then, you must bring yourself up to speed on the old task before you get started again.

Dumb and Dumber

According to *USA Today*, each time you shift from one task to another and back again, you burn up a certain amount of brain energy and intelligence. At the end of a busy day of multitasking, you can lose as many as ten IQ points. So, you become progressively dumber throughout the day, ending the day feeling burned out and often indecisive about the smallest things, such as what you want to have for dinner or watch on television that evening.

Multitasking is tempting, but it is an insidious use of time. It can actually sabotage your career and undermine your ability to accomplish the most important tasks upon which all your success depends.

Decide to Concentrate

Resolve today to make it a habit to plan your work carefully, set priorities, and then begin on your most important task. Once you have begun on your top task or output, resolve that you will work single-mindedly, without diversion or distraction, until that task is complete.

One of the techniques used by highly productive executives is to work at home in the morning or evening, or on the weekend, when you can concentrate single-mindedly without interruption of any kind.

Another key to single-minded concentration is to avoid the "attraction of distraction." Instead of responding to every e-mail or ring on your phone, "leave things off!" Close your door, turn off all your devices, and put everything aside so that you can work on the one task that can make the greatest difference to your company and your career at this point. When you make this a habit, your productivity, performance, and output will double and triple, almost overnight.

THIRTEEN

Overcome Procrastination

IT HAS BEEN SAID that "procrastination is the thief of time." A wise man in one of my seminars expanded on that by saying, "Procrastination is the thief of life."

Your ability to overcome procrastination and to get the job done on schedule can make all the difference between success and failure in your career.

However, the fact is that everyone procrastinates. Everyone has too much to do and too little time. But if everyone procrastinates, what is the difference between the high producer and the low producer?

Simple. The *high producer* procrastinates on tasks and activities of low or no value. The *low producer* procrastinates on tasks that have considerable value to the company and to the individual's own career. For you to produce at your maximum, you must resolve to engage in "creative procrastination" from this day forward.

Consciously and deliberately decide which tasks you are going to put off. Look at your list of work for the day and choose those items that you are not going to do until you have completed other items that are vastly more important. You must work consciously and deliberately instead of procrastinating accidentally and automatically.

We always tend to procrastinate on our biggest tasks, which are usually our highest-value tasks as well. There are a series of techniques that you can use to overcome or at least manage procrastination. In fact, there are libraries full of books, one or two of them written by myself, on the subject of overcoming procrastination. Here are some good ideas that you should start with right away.

Mental Programming

"Do it now!"

These are perhaps the most powerful words you can use to increase your productivity. Whenever you find yourself procrastinating on an important task, repeat to yourself, with energy and enthusiasm, "Do it now! Do it now! Do it now!"

The amazing discovery is that after you have repeated these words ten, twenty, or even a hundred times, you will find yourself unconsciously impelled to stay on your most important task and complete that job before you do anything else.

Completing Larger Tasks

Henry Ford once wrote, "Any goal can be achieved if you break it down into enough small parts."

Any big task that you have to complete can be completed if you break it down into enough small parts. One of the best techniques of all is to divide your task into "bite-size pieces." Take a piece of paper and write down every small part of the task that you have to do, in sequence, from the first little job to the final job that completes the task.

Then, discipline yourself to do "number one" on your list. Sometimes, the decision to take action on the first step on a large task makes it easier for you to do the next step, and the next step, and the next step as well. Sometimes just forcing yourself to start on a major task will help you to develop the momentum and energy necessary to work right through until the task is complete.

The Salami Slice Method

A variation of the "bite-size pieces" technique for overcoming procrastination is called the "salami slice method." Just as you would not try to eat a loaf of salami in one bite, you do not try to do a large task in one time period. Instead, you salami-slice the task; you reduce the size of the task by slicing off one small part at a time. You then resolve to complete that one small part before you go on to something else.

Each time you sit down with your major task, especially if you are overwhelmed with other pressing responsibilities, resolve to complete one part of the task at a time. Often this strategy will get you started on the project and make it easier to complete parts two, three, four, and so on.

Develop a Sense of Urgency

One of the rarest and most valuable human qualities in the world of work is a sense of urgency. It is estimated that only about 2 percent of people move quickly to get the job done. When you develop a reputation for having an "action orientation" and for getting the job done quickly, you'll move onto the fast track in your career.

When 300 chief executive officers were asked what employees could do to put themselves on the fast track in their corporations, 85 percent of the top executives had the same reply. The most important qualities that they looked for were 1) the ability to set priorities and 2) the ability to start on the most important job and get it done quickly and well.

When you develop a reputation for starting on your most important tasks and completing them quickly and well, you will be happily surprised at all the wonderful opportunities that will open up for you.

FOURTEEN

Create Blocks of Time

YOU REQUIRE UNBROKEN blocks of time for maximum accomplishment. The more important your work is, the more important it becomes for you to establish blocks of time to work on serious projects.

You need a minimum of sixty to ninety minutes to accomplish anything worthwhile. It takes about thirty minutes just to get your mind into a complex task, like preparing a proposal, report, or even planning an important project. Once you are into the task, you can then concentrate single-mindedly, at a high level of awareness and creativity for the next sixty minutes or more of serious, focused work.

Don't Mix Creative and Administrative

You cannot mix creative tasks with functional or administrative tasks. You cannot really do operational tasks and creative tasks simultaneously. They require fast or slow thinking, but not both. Office activities require fast, short-term thinking. Creative tasks require thought, planning, and application.

Think of creative time as your "internal prime time" and operational time as your "external prime time." And don't mix them up. You cannot do big creative jobs requiring focus and concentration in a typical office environment unless you put up a Do Not Disturb sign on that door. Otherwise, you must be creative in finding ways to get away from your work environment so that you can complete the tasks that your career really depends on.

How to Create Chunks of Time

Here are several recommendations for creating blocks of time, any one of which can dramatically improve your effectiveness and efficiency.

First, work in the morning when you are the freshest and most alert. Many of the most productive people in business discipline themselves to go to bed early and then arise at 5:00 or 6:00 A.M. so that they can work for sixty to ninety minutes uninterrupted before they go into the office. Even if you get into the office a bit late, in those ninety minutes of uninterrupted work, you will accomplish as much as the average person does in an office environment in three hours.

Another time that you can use to your advantage is lunchtime. This is a great opportunity for you to shut off your phone, turn off your Internet connection, and remove other distractions while everyone else is out of the office having lunch. You'll have sixty straight minutes of peace and quiet where you can work single-mindedly to clear up some of your most important tasks.

Do Not Disturb

Another strategy you can use is to close your office door for certain periods each day during which you work single-mindedly on your biggest tasks. Many executives will get a Do Not Disturb sign from a hotel and hang it on their door handle at work. Everyone knows that while this sign is on the door, no one is allowed to interrupt them except in the case of a real emergency.

My controller, a talented and skilled woman, complained to me that she was overwhelmed with nonstop interruptions from different people. As a result, she was unable to get her detailed accounting work done and send out her financial statements and reports on schedule. After I recommended that she put a Do Not Disturb sign on her door and work nonstop for one hour in the morning and one hour in the afternoon without interruptions, it transformed her work life. She told me afterward that, within a few days, she was totally caught up. Even more, none of those interruptions turned out to be so important that they couldn't wait for a later time.

Gain Extra Hours

Here is yet another great technique that virtually all executives on the fast track use. It is so simple that it should be illegal. Get up a little earlier and arrive at your office one hour before everyone else. Use that hour to organize your day and to get started before there are any possible interruptions. Then work through lunch and gain one more hour of productivity. Finally, stay one hour later, after everyone else has gone home, and use that time to wrap up your day and complete your most important tasks.

This is an amazing technique! By adjusting your day in this way, you beat the traffic on your way to work and you beat the traffic on the way home. In between, you add three productive hours to each working day. You accomplish two, three, or even five times as much as the average person who works regular hours. With this strategy, you can double your output and transform your career.

Remember, you are a potential genius. One of the areas where you can demonstrate your creativity is in creating blocks of time when you can get more done and start moving ahead faster in your career.

FIFTEEN

Control Interruptions

UNEXPECTED AND unscheduled interruptions are among the biggest time wasters in business and industry. These interruptions can be in the form of a bell going off on your computer, a telephone ringing, an SMS message coming in on your smartphone, or people just walking into your office because they need to talk.

It turns out that people are the greatest time wasters in the world of work. As much as 50 percent of time at work is spent in idle chitchat with coworkers. Many people come into work in the morning and begin chitchatting with their coworkers, and then continue for the next two or three hours. In many environments, people don't really start serious work until about 11:00 a.m., and then soon it is time to break for lunch. After lunch, they come back and chitchat with their coworkers some more, not getting back into the job until 1:30 or 2:00 p.m.

Work All the Time You Work

The rule for you is to "work all the time you work." When you go into your workplace, begin work immediately. Do not chat with others, read the newspaper, or surf the Internet. Since you planned out your day the evening before, you begin immediately on your most important task, and keep working, task by task, until you get your most important jobs done.

Minimize Interruptions

When someone phones you, cut to the chase immediately. Say something like, "Hello, Bill. It's nice to hear your voice. What can I do for you?"

Get right to the point. Don't waste time. Before you call Bill, quickly write out an agenda of the points you want to cover in your phone call. When you get Bill on the line, you say, "I know how busy you are. I have three points that I need to go over with you and then I will let you get back to work."

This approach is both polite and professional. Most busy businesspeople are going to appreciate your getting to the point quickly and then getting off the phone.

When someone comes into your office to chat, you can say, "I would love to talk with you right now, but I really have to get back to work. I have to complete this task by this afternoon."

Whenever you say those magic words, "I have to get back to work," the other person will pack up and leave.

Stand Up Immediately

To minimize the time cost of unexpected interruptions, when someone comes into your office, stand up and approach the other person saying something like, "I was just on my way out. What can I do for you?"

Then, you walk with the person out of your office and back into the hallway, talking and listening. When the person has finished talking, you then let him go back to his work, and you return to your office and your work.

Another technique is to take outside visitors to a separate meeting room rather than bringing them into your office. Then, you politely set a time limit at the beginning of the discussion by saying something such as, "I have an important call coming in from our agent in London at exactly 3:15. I can't get out of that appointment. I'm sure we can cover everything we need to cover by that time."

In his book *The Effective Executive*, Peter Drucker makes the point that not only do people waste your time, but you waste the time of other people. He suggests that you have the courage to go and ask other people, "What do I do that wastes your time?" When you invite people to be perfectly honest with you in answering this question, you will be quite amazed at the ideas you'll hear to help increase their efficiency and effectiveness, and your own as well.

SIXTEEN

Batch Your Tasks

BATCHING YOUR tasks simply means doing similar things at the same time. There's a "learning curve" in everything you do. When you complete a series of similar or identical tasks all in a row, the learning curve allows you to reduce the time required to complete each task by as much as 80 percent by the time you complete the fifth identical task.

For example, in writing letters and correspondence or answering e-mail, you bundle them all together and do them at the same time.

You batch your telephone calls and return them all in a row. If you have to interview a number of people, interview them consecutively, one after another. Do all your similar tasks at the same time rather than doing a little bit now and a little bit later.

Use E-Mail as a Servant

How you deal with your e-mail is going to have a major impact on your career. There are some people who are slaves to their e-mail. They have a bell that goes off each time a new e-mail comes in, and whatever they are doing, they turn immediately to their inbox to check on the message. In effect, they "switch tasks" and then return to what it was they were doing, immediately losing momentum, clarity, and output in their most important tasks.

Tim Ferris, in his bestselling book *The 4-Hour Workweek*, explains how he went from being a slave to his e-mail twelve to fourteen hours a day to mastering the process completely.

First, he decided to only answer his e-mail twice a day, at eleven o'clock in the morning and four in the afternoon. Then he went from twice a day to once a day, to once a week. Even when answering e-mails once a week, his efficiency, effectiveness, productivity, and income increased.

Julie Morgenstern, the time management expert, wrote a book called *Never Check E-Mail in the Morning*. This title and the very idea come as a shock to most people.

They Can Wait

Some of the most productive people I know have an automatic response on their e-mail. It reads something like this: "I only answer my e-mail twice a day because of my busy schedule. If you have sent me an e-mail, I will get back to you as soon as I possibly can. If this is an emergency, call this number and speak to this person."

A busy journalist told the story of going to Europe for two weeks. His e-mail was inaccessible for the entire time. When he returned, he had more than 700 messages waiting for him. He knew that it would take him many hours, even several days, to go through 700 e-mails. So he took a deep breath and pressed "delete all."

His attitude was simple. He said, "I refuse to be the slave of any person who sends me an e-mail, expecting me to reply immediately. Besides, if any of these e-mails were important, whoever sent the e-mail will send it again."

And he was right; 90 percent of the e-mails that he deleted were never repeated, and the ones that he deleted that were important ones were resent within a few days.

Make a decision not to allow your e-mail to control your life, like the tail wagging the dog. Instead, discipline yourself to use e-mail as a business tool. Make your responses quick and to the point. Check your e-mail only twice a day, or less frequently. Even better, leave your e-mail off on the weekends and spend more time with your family and friends or engaged in personal activities.

The good news is that you will probably never miss an important message. There are very few things that happen that cannot wait another day or two, especially in business.

SEVENTEEN

Manage the Telephone

THE TELEPHONE CAN be an excellent servant or a terrible master—especially if you feel compelled to answer whenever it rings. To achieve maximum productivity, you must put the telephone in its place so that you do not end up a slave to anyone who dials your number.

The best way to get control of your telephone calls is to have all of them screened by your administrative assistant; otherwise, put your phone on silent and let calls go to your voice mail. There are few calls or messages that cannot wait until it is more convenient for you to turn your attention to dealing with them.

One of the reasons that we are becoming slaves to the attraction of distraction is *curiosity*. We can't stop ourselves from wondering who is sending us a message, or who is on the other end of the phone. The only way to resist this temptation to be distracted is for you to turn off the phone completely so that you don't even hear it ring.

Whenever you are meeting with staff and subordinates, or with your boss or with clients, have your calls held. Turn off your cell phone. Allow no interruptions whatsoever. There is seldom anything so important that it will not wait.

Ten minutes of uninterrupted time in conversation with another individual will be more productive than thirty or forty minutes with the phone ringing and being answered throughout your conversation. Later, you can call people back, one after another.

Bunch Your Calls

If you have to make a series of phone calls in the course of the day, make them all at the same time. Carve out a chunk of time where you can turn off every other distraction and only make phone calls to the important people on your list. Write down the name, number, and subject of each person that you need to call.

Schedule phone calls as religiously as you would schedule a meeting with your boss. If it is an important call, write out your agenda for the call so that you are working from a list when you are talking to the other person. There are few things as exasperating as getting off an important phone call with a difficult-to-reach person and discovering that you have forgotten to cover an important point because you didn't write it down.

Be Polite and Professional

When you call another person, always ask, "Is this a good time to talk?" Top executives use this polite and professional phrase to open up a phone call, even prearranged, scheduled phone calls. If an emergency has arisen in the interim, it may not be a good time to talk, after all. If you try to forge ahead with your conversation at that point, the other person will be unable to pay close attention. So always ask, "Is this a good time?"

If the other person says it is not a good time, offer to call back later or ask the person to suggest a time that would be more convenient. This is a simple way to show courtesy and respect, and it will be appreciated. Never assume that the other person has the time to talk to you at this moment, no matter what you have arranged earlier.

Avoid Telephone Tag

Do everything possible to avoid playing telephone tag. Set up telephone appointments exactly as you would set up a face-to-face meeting in the office. When you call people, leave a specific time and number at which you would be available. When people call you, and you can't always speak with them, have your secretary get a call-back time that is convenient for the caller. It should be during hours when you will be in your office or available by telephone so that you can return calls on time.

Use the telephone as a business tool. Get on and off the phone quickly. Get straight to the point. Be polite and friendly, but businesslike and result-oriented.

The more precise and prepared you can be about the time and content of your telephone conversation, the more you will get done, faster, and the more productive you will be in every call.

EIGHTEEN

Conduct Effective Meetings

FULLY 25 PERCENT to 50 percent of management time is spent in meetings of all kinds. These may be one-on-one meetings, brief meetings in the hallway or while going in and out of the office, or more formal sit-down meetings in an office or a meeting room. Unfortunately, 50 percent or more of meeting time is wasted. Meetings consume enormous amounts of time and produce little lasting value. However, meetings are also a key management tool and must be used effectively.

Calculate the Meeting Cost

Make sure that you have a good reason for calling or attending any meeting. Look upon each meeting as a business investment. Look upon a meeting as carrying a cost in managerial and staff time and wages. Take the combined hourly pay of the people in those meetings and realize that you need to get a return on your investment of this amount of money.

If you have ten people in a room who earn an average of $50 per hour, then it is going to cost $500 out of the bank account of the company for a one-hour meeting. If someone wanted to spend $500 on a project and came to you for approval, you would want to know what the company would get from this expense. You would probably want to think about it for a while before you approved it. You might even demand more information and details before you are comfortable authorizing an expenditure of this size. Treat each meeting the same way.

Avoid unnecessary meetings. Always ask if this meeting has to be held at all. Whenever a meeting is unnecessary, it is necessary *not* to have the meeting. If you personally don't need to attend the meeting, then don't attend. If you are organizing the meeting, ask yourself who is essential to the meeting, and invite only those people. Refrain from inviting people who don't need to be there just to make them feel good or important.

Prepare an Agenda

Prepare an agenda for every meeting, and always follow a written agenda. Prioritize the items on the agenda and deal with the most important ones first, in case you run out of time. As the meeting leader, your job is to keep the discussion on track and push for closure on each item before moving on.

Start and stop your meetings on time. If you have people who are chronically late, you might consider locking the door shortly after your start time. Another strategy is to assume that the latecomer is not coming at all and just begin the meeting. Once the meeting begins, ensure that there will be no interruptions while you are in the meeting.

In his bestselling book *What Got You Here Won't Get You There*, Marshall Goldsmith says that one of the biggest flaws in leadership is the tendency to dominate meetings that are attended by the leader's subordinates. Because you are the boss, everyone listens when you speak. Over time, people learn not to say anything or to interrupt, but just to let you continue speaking as long as you want, on any subject that you want.

Ask More Questions

In a meeting, be like the wise old owl that has two ears and one mouth. Use your ears and your mouth in exactly that proportion. Ask more questions and listen more closely than you talk or contribute to the agenda. Use a meeting to elicit the very best thinking of each person in the room, which is not possible if you are talking all the time.

The best and most efficient meetings are stand-up meetings. You can hold this type of meeting, perhaps in your office, only no one sits down and whatever needs to be discussed is discussed quickly and succinctly so that everyone can get back to work.

It's simple to convene such a meeting. You say, "In the interest of time—because I know how busy everyone is—let's hold a stand-up meeting. That way we can cover everything and get back to work faster." Since people usually are busy, you will find that, given the right time and place, this type of meeting is very much appreciated by your staff members.

As Peter Drucker once wrote, "Anything more than 25 percent of managerial time spent in meetings is a sign of malorganization."

NINETEEN

Read Faster, Remember More

THE AVERAGE businessperson today is reading thousands of words of e-mails, reports, news stories, business information, magazine articles, and other data. To be successful today, you have to keep current with your reading requirements. We live in a knowledge-based society, and one key piece of information can have an immediate effect on your work and your decision making.

Take some time to be selective about what you read. The best time saver in the world of reading and keeping current is the Delete button on your keyboard. Use it early and use it often. Resist the temptation to spend time reading things that are not of immediate value or relevance to your life and work.

Learn to Speed-Read

You cannot avoid all of the incoming information, but you can sort it and go through it at a time and place that makes sense to you. One of the most important skills you can develop is to learn to speed-read. If you have never taken a course in speed-reading, you should do it now. This one course will allow you to triple your reading speed and level of retention, probably in the first two lessons. The technologies that have developed in speed-reading are quite phenomenal, and anyone can learn how to read 500 to 1,000 words per minute with high levels of comprehension.

Bunch Your Reading

When you come across valuable items, summaries, or pieces of information on the Internet, print them out and put them into a file, or put them aside in a separate digital file on your computer for reading later. Instead of "task-shifting"—that is, switching away from the work that you are doing to read a recent piece of information—put it aside to read at a later time. Once you get into the habit of doing this, you will be amazed at how much more you read, and how much more attention you can give when you do read that material.

With regard to newspapers especially, you can either have the most important information published in newspapers come to your computer on a daily basis, or you can read the paper version. In either case, skim quickly and read only what is relevant to you. In news reporting, the most important information is usually in the headline and the first paragraph. Very often, you do not need to read all the details in the story to understand exactly what has happened.

Read Selectively

Magazines are designed and crafted in a way to get you to read through the magazine page by page. This is so that you will get the maximum exposure to the advertisements in the magazines. (It's the same with newspapers.)

For this reason, you must read magazines, journals, newspapers, and newsletters selectively, reading only what is relevant and important to you. Review the table of contents and go straight to the articles of interest to your life and work. A great technique for printed materials is called "rip and read." Rip out the articles that you want to read, put them in a file, and carry the file with you to be referred to later, when you have "downtime."

Review books carefully before deciding which ones you want to spend time reading. You can subscribe to book review services, both in print and online, and get the very best ideas from any book in just a few minutes.

Just Say No

The best way to save time in your reading endeavors is to make a decision not to read something at all. By carefully screening the material's foreword, table of contents, the introduction and information about the author, or the index, you may find that the book or journal is not of importance to you. In that case, discontinue reading or discard it completely so that you can free up more time to do things of greater importance.

Develop a System

Over the years, I have developed the rhythm and habit of reading three or more hours each day on subjects related to business, economics, politics, and personal development. That amounts to more than 150,000 hours of reading over the course of my career. With the information that I accumulated, I have been able to write more than sixty books, including this one.

When people ask me how it is that I can read so much, my explanation is simple. I organize my reading and work away at it a little bit at a time, minute by minute, hour by hour, flight by flight, and whenever I have a period of free time, such as in an airport lounge waiting for a plane.

Remember, "readers are leaders." It is not possible for you to keep current with your field and be on top of your industry unless you are feeding your mind, continually but selectively, with the information that is being generated today by some of the smartest people who ever lived.

TWENTY

Invest in Personal Development

THE MOST IMPORTANT thing you do to increase your value, improve your results, and make yourself more important to your business is to become better and better at the most important things you do.

Self-development must be an ongoing and continuous part of your time usage every day. It is a key time management function that can put you on the path to the executive suite and beyond.

Find the time within your schedule to continue growing and developing. The basic rule with regard to personal development is that you can go no further than you have gone today with your current knowledge and skill. To go further and advance your career, you have to gain more knowledge. You have to learn more to earn more.

Continuous and Never-Ending Improvement

Work on developing and improving yourself every day. If you were to read something for one hour a day that improved your ability to do your work, that would put you in the top one percent in our society within five years.

Listen to educational audio programs when you are traveling in your car. Today, virtually all of the finest information and ideas that have ever been assembled in English, or in any language, are available as audio recordings on CDs or downloads to a smartphone or tablet.

The average commuter spends 500 to 1,000 hours per year in the car. That's twelve or twenty forty-hour weeks, which is equivalent to one or two university semesters. This means that you can get the benefit of almost full-time university attendance by simply turning traveling time into learning time. If you are not listening to audio programs in your car or when traveling, you are missing out on one of the great learning opportunities that exist today.

Attend Seminars Taught by Experts

Attend seminars and workshops given by experts in your field at least four times a year. Be aggressive about seeking out these seminars. Be prepared to travel large distances to learn from the very best people in your business.

The key is for you to attend seminars taught by people with practical experience who have already achieved success in their field. Try to avoid lectures and seminars from university professors who write from their ivory towers. They have seldom been in the trenches, and what they teach tends to be academically correct but practically useless. There is almost no way that you can apply their ideas to get better results in your work.

TWENTY-ONE

Organize Your Work Space

ONE OF THE GREAT time management tools is to work from a clean desk and in an organized work space. Just as an excellent chef cleans up the kitchen before and after cooking, you should organize your work space completely before you begin your work. One of the most successful entrepreneurs in recent history said that the key to his success was to "always work from a clean desk."

Peter Drucker observed that effective executives always have a clean desk. Everything except the one thing that they are working on at the moment has been removed and put away, which is why they are able to focus with greater clarity and get more done, of higher quality, in a shorter period of time.

Put all of your documents away in the appropriate files, both physical and online. Deal only with your current task. Try to have only one item in front of you whenever possible.

The top professionals in every field keep a tidy and highly ordered work space at all times. Think of a carpenter, dentist, or doctor. They clean up and reorganize as they go through their day.

Get organized and stay organized. Make sure your office supplies and materials are fully stocked and available at hand. You will find that nothing is more destructive to efficiency and effectiveness than having to start a job and then stop, and then start again, for lack of proper preparation or supplies.

Organization Increases Productivity

Many people believe that they work more effectively in a messy work environment with a cluttered desk. Yet every study that has been done with people shows that when they are forced to clean up their work environment so that they have only one task in front of them, their productivity doubles and triples, usually overnight.

People who work with cluttered desks are found to spend an enormous amount of each working day looking for the materials they need among the clutter around them. Psychologically, the sight of a cluttered desk or office provides subconscious feedback that reinforces your perception that you are disorganized. It leads to continuous distraction as your eyes and your attention dart from item to item, and back again.

Conclusion

THE FINAL POINT about time management is the concept of balance. The most important thing that you can instill in your life is balance and moderation. By practicing the methods, ideas, and techniques in this book, you will become a master time manager, and have more time for your family and your personal life.

Often, people take time management programs so that they can increase the number of things that they can do on a day-to-day basis. However, as the wise man said, "There is more to life than simply increasing its speed."

The main purpose of learning and practicing time management skills is to enhance and improve the overall quality of your life. It is to increase the amount of pleasure and happiness you experience.

Your Quality of Life

No matter how appropriate your job is for you, the quality of your life is going to be largely determined by three things. The first is the quality of your *inner life*: how well you get along with yourself, how much you like yourself, and how good you feel about your character and personality. Inner development takes time and reflection, plus reading and thinking about the great questions of life.

The second area is your *health*. No amount of success will compensate for ill health. Take time to eat the right foods, exercise regularly, and get proper rest and recreation. Sometimes, the best use of your time is to go to bed early and get a good night's sleep.

Finally, and most important of all, take time for your *relationships*. The people you care about and who care about you are the most critical factors in your life. Never allow yourself to get so caught up in your work that you ignore the primacy of those key relationships with your spouse, children, and close friends.

A great life is one that is in balance. If you spend sufficient time preserving and enhancing the quality of your relationships, you will find that you get more joy, satisfaction, and fulfillment out of your work; you'll find success.

A wise old doctor once observed, "I never spoke to a businessman on his deathbed who said that he wished he had spent more time in the office."

Thank you, and good luck in using these ideas in every part of your life.

ABOUT THE AUTHOR

Brian Tracy is a professional speaker, trainer, seminar leader, and consultant, and chairman of Brian Tracy International, a training and consulting company based in Solana Beach, California.

Brian bootstrapped his way to success. In 1981, in talks and seminars around the U.S., he began teaching the principles he forged in sales and business. Today, his books and audio and video programs—more than 500 of them—are available in 38 languages and are used in 55 countries.

He is the bestselling author of more than fifty books, including *Full Engagement* and *Reinvention*.

"Inspiring, entertaining, informative, motivational..."

Brian Tracy is one of the world's top speakers. He addresses more than 250,000 people annually—in over 100 appearances—and has consulted and trained at more than 1,000 corporations. In his career he has reached over five million people in 58 countries. He has lived and practiced every principle in his writing and speeches:

21st-Century Thinking: How to outmaneuver the competition and get superior results in an ever-turbulent business climate.

Leadership in the New Millennium: Learn the most powerful leadership principles—ever—to get maximum results, faster.

Advanced Selling Strategies: How to use modern sales' most advanced strategies and tactics to outperform your competitors.

The Psychology of Success: Think and act like the top performers. Learn practical, proven techniques for excellence.

To book Brian to speak at your next meeting or conference, visit Brian Tracy International at www.briantracy.com, or call (858) 436-7316 for a free promotional package. Brian will carefully customize his talk to your specific needs.